SEASONS

Winter

by Ann Herriges

BELLWETHER MEDIA • MINNEAPOLIS, MN

Note to Librarians, Teachers, and Parents:

Blastoff! Readers are carefully developed by literacy experts and combine standards-based content with developmentally appropriate text.

Level 1 provides the most support through repetition of high-frequency words, light text, predictable sentence patterns, and strong visual support.

Level 2 offers early readers a bit more challenge through varied simple sentences, increased text load, and less repetition of high-frequency words.

Level 3 advances early-fluent readers toward fluency through increased text and concept load, less reliance on visuals, longer sentences, and more literary language.

Whichever book is right for your reader, Blastoff! Readers are the perfect books to build confidence and encourage a love of reading that will last a lifetime!

This edition first published in 2007 by Bellwether Media.

No part of this publication may be reproduced in whole or in part without written permission of the publisher. For information regarding permission, write to Bellwether Media Inc., Attention: Permissions Department, Post Office Box 1C, Minnetonka, MN 55345-9998.

Library of Congress Cataloging-in-Publication Data
Herriges, Ann.
  Winter / by Ann Herriges.
    p. cm. — (Seasons) (Blastoff! readers)
Summary: "Simple text and supportive images introduce beginning readers to the characteristics of the season of winter. Intended for students in kindergarten through third grade."
  Includes bibliographical references and index.
  ISBN-10: 1-60014-030-0 (hardcover : alk. paper)
  ISBN-13: 978-1-60014-030-3 (hardcover : alk. paper)
  1. Winter—Juvenile literature. I. Title. II. Series.

  QB637.8.H47 2007
  508.2—dc22   2006000611

Text copyright © 2007 by Bellwether Media.
Printed in the United States of America.

Table of Contents

Winter is the **season** that comes after fall. Winter is different all around the world.

Some places are very cold in winter. But other places can be hot!

In cold places, the air is **frosty**.
You can see your breath.

The ground **freezes**. Lakes and ponds freeze too.

Snow falls when the air is cold.

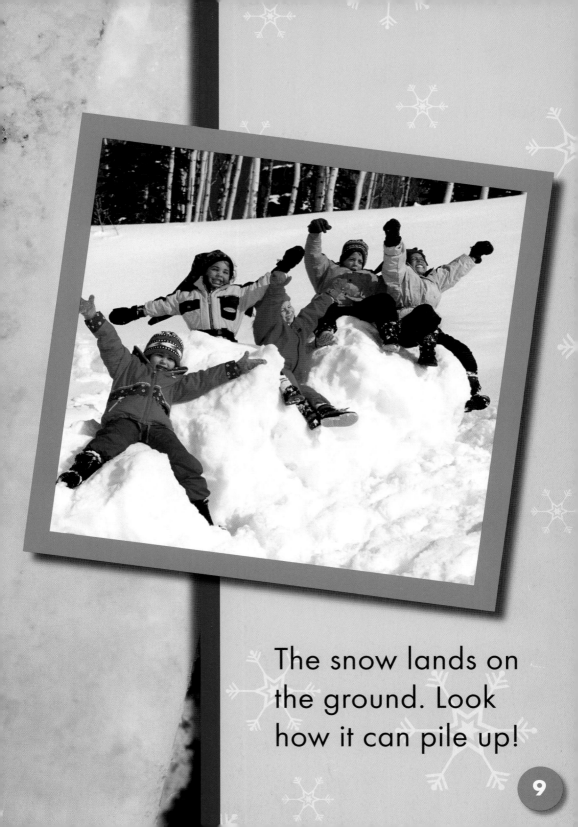

The snow lands on
the ground. Look
how it can pile up!

Winter can bring a **blizzard**. Heavy snow falls.

10

Icy wind blows the snow around. It is hard to see in a blizzard.

The sun is low in the sky in winter. **Shadows** are long.

There is not much daylight in winter. It gets dark before dinnertime.

Plants stop growing in winter.
Some trees lose their leaves.

Deer eat small twigs from trees and shrubs. Squirrels eat the nuts they hid in fall.

Some animals grow thicker fur to keep them warm. Sometimes the fur even changes color to match the snow.

Some animals sleep through
the winter. Bats sleep close
together in caves.

Mice sleep in **burrows**. Snakes and turtles sleep deep underground.

It is fun to play outside in winter.
Put on your coat, boots, hat,
and mittens!

The winter snow is good
for **sledding**, **skiing**, and
making snowpeople.

At the end of winter the air feels warmer. Snow starts to melt. **Icicles** go *drip, drip, drip.* Spring is almost here!

Glossary

blizzard—a strong snowstorm; blizzards have heavy snowfall, low temperatures, and strong winds.

burrow—a hole or tunnel dug in the ground by a small animal

freeze—to become solid; water turns to ice when the temperature is 32 degrees Fahrenheit (0 degrees Celsius).

frosty—very cold

icicle—a long, pointed stem of ice that forms when dripping water freezes

season—one of the four parts of the year; the seasons are spring, summer, fall, and winter.

shadow—a dark shape made by an object blocking out the sun

skiing—to glide across the snow on skis

sledding—to ride down a hill on a sled

snow—ice crystals that fall from clouds

To Learn More

AT THE LIBRARY

Florian, Douglas. *Winter Eyes*. New York: Green Willow Books, 1999.

Gibbons, Gail. *The Reasons for Seasons*. New York: Holiday House, 1995.

Glaser, Linda. *It's Winter*. Brookfield, Conn.: Millbrook Press, 2002.

Hader, Berta. *The Big Snow*. New York: Aladdin, 2005.

Pfeffer, Wendy. *The Shortest Day: Celebrating the Winter Solstice*. New York: Dutton, 2003.

Rockwell, Anne. *Four Seasons Make a Year*. New York: Walker, 2004.

Van Laan, Nancy. *When Winter Comes*. New York: Atheneum, 2000.

ON THE WEB

Learning more about the seasons is as easy as 1, 2, 3.

1. Go to www.factsurfer.com

2. Enter "seasons" into search box.

3. Click the "Surf" button and you will see a list of related web sites.

With factsurfer.com, finding more information is just a click away.

Index

The photographs in this book are reproduced through the courtesy of: Comstock, front cover, pp. 4, 8-9, 12, 13, 14, 20 (all), 21; Elyse Lewin/Getty Images, p. 5; Harald Sund/Getty Images, pp. 6-7; Richard Price/Getty Images, p. 9; Rob Atkins/Getty Images, pp. 10-11; James Gritz/Getty Images, p. 15; Michael S Quinton/Getty Images, pp. 16, 19; Andrea Pistolesi/Getty Images, p. 17; Tim Shepard-Oxford Scientific Films/Getty Images, p. 18.